THROUGH
THE SHADOWS

Through the Shadows

Carroll Blair

Aveon Publishing Company

ISBN: 978-1-936430-30-7

Library of Congress Control Number
2016916351

Aveon Publishing Co.
P.O. Box 380739
Cambridge, MA 02238-0739 USA

Also by Carroll Blair

Grains of Thought
Facing the Circle
Reel to Real
Shifting Tides
Reaches
Out of Silence
Quarter Notes
By Rays of Light
Into the Inner Life
Gnosis of the Heart
Soul Reflections
Beneath and Beyond the Surface
Of Courage and Commitment
For Today and Tomorrow
In Meditation
Sightings Along the Journey
Through Desert's Fire
Offerings to Pilgrims
Human Natures
(Of Animal and Spiritual)
Atoms from the Suns of Solitude
Colors of Devotion
Voicings

Contents

In Aloneness

Usually alone am I
and usually glad to
be alone, and productive
when I'm alone
and always at my best
when I am alone,
and never more focused
nor of greater resolve
than when I am alone,
and the measure of a life's
worth is in what it delivers —
contributes — creates —
[is the fruit of that life]
and I stand in my aloneness
and let the world be the
judge of its account —

Through the Shadows

Moving through the shadows where
nothing grows, time and space still
accommodate the sphere where the
ventureless wait for life to happen —
yet it is life that is always waiting, even
while happening . . . turn a corner, and
it is there — in every motion, at every
pause, it waits . . . waits for you to emerge
from the shadows — to begin to engage,
to grow . . . to go to where it longs to
take you —

Life Whispers

The world is ever saying: "Let me take you for a ride, keep you on the spin" . . . but Life whispers: "I have something better for you than the round and round of this world . . . . Are you in?"

The Temporal

The temporal is full of fear —
it sleeps with one eye open, guarding
its treasure [its wares] destined for
dust — ever afraid of loss, ever
avoiding the facing of death, getting
no deeper than the frivolous and
caring for no better as life fades,
as time passes, sweeping those along
who resign themselves to go along —

From the Start

What falls to dust is
doomed from the start
and what is doomed from
the start isn't worth starting

To Not Ignore

To have courage for the hints from life;
to not ignore these carriers of truth . . .
like needles puncturing the skin
[the spiritual skin] prodding us to
take things as they are and not what
we would like them to be; to refuse the
temptation of Façade, suggesting much,
though offering only the false for the
acceptance of what it pretends to be of
the genuine, taking away so much more
than what it gives to those who are taken
by its allure . . . oh how much to be saved,
the countless traps to be avoided by
opening up to those hints from life,
offering guidance of the invaluable
for life —

Never to Recognize

What some are looking for is really nothing
[objectively nothing] but they don't recognize
that it is nothing, and when happening upon
Something there's no realization [no cognitive
computation] of what they've encountered
and see it as being nothing and go on looking
and not finding, and never discerning the
truth of it all . . . and some look to something
more, but do not move — some move
toward what is more, but only a step or
two — some go further — and some [few]
go far enough that their journey within
can no longer be tracked — but most don't
even bother to look beyond the follies of the
day-to-day that they wake to each morning
[each day] and believe themselves to be waking
to life — going from cradle to grave never to
recognize this Folly of all follies —

Like Bricks of Air

Lessons are taught and not learned
or learned but not heeded
and things that need to be changed
don't change, and what needs to be
stabilized is destroyed, rebuilt, destroyed
again, and the hours are stacked like
bricks of air creating nothing
holding nothing, showing nothing
as darkness continues to envelop light
as blackboards continue to be
turned to gray walls
as time devastates the myth
of lasting glory

Through the Fog

There was no one standing to say
Yes that day, calling for conviction
before the promise went sour . . .
lanterns lit through the fog without
cover of nightfall, blanketing more
area than was needed to raise the
breathing but not yet living, the
streets readied to be walked and
preyed upon as creatures coated
in fur sat waiting on empty houses
watching the sale of Yes coming in,
sailing through the fog . . .

There Not

Where new life is not allowed to breathe
and cornerstones turn to tombstones,
and piercings of light are arrested by
rays of darkness, and railways are banned
from the entrance to all stations and
pronouncements of the commitment to
love are made barren, and the clock is
countered that wants to move forward
and streams of red mix with matter of
brown breaking the wave before it comes,
halting the call for fortune to arrive
and grace to be, and tidings to be made
glad long covered in foils of waste and
to let fire be fire, and beauty, beauty
and not fear the alarm, to bring on
the hurt that will close out the harm
able to pave the way to the sublime
where such is out of reach in the day-
to-day show of the fleeting —

For Something More

Something more than the sellers of the day,
than the runners of the night, than the
hollowing out of culture from the inside out;
more than the trials that pass for noble
without real test or challenge, and the dream
for a life fulfilled without paying the price;
and more, than the retreats taken for advance,
and the leaders without even the courage of
the last to follow; in need of more than the
baseness given virtual wings to raise the
illusion of ascent, and the marches for justice
that cease to step when the sun fades and
cameras are shut away; than the indifference
that bears the mark of doom, and the laughter
veiling the cries of the earth not being heard . . .
and may there be more [now more] than the
hope for the shattering of false hope and for
truth to be told where it has yet to be told amid
the myriad of woes caused by bandits that can
no longer be shamed or shaken from the villainy
of their crimes, aided by an ignorance held even
among those on the side of the good adhering
to boundaries created by the dead of long ago
and the allegiance to ways that have gone to
expiration, waiting for a hero to bear all at the
exit of his deed as the hand of fate grows numb

and the gods walk away from it all, leaving the
story unattended and the promise of tomorrow
that tomorrow never gave —

Of the Same Source

What is behind the mad breakout
of war and the slumbering trance
of a bourgeois peace is the same
menacing life-killing beast —

One is when it's awake —
the other, asleep

The Race

Every day the world is off and
running with many millions
entering their lives in the race,
but where are they going and
what are they not yet doing
that they will do when they
never get there . . .

What Gives

What gives with all this taking
and taking and tripling down on
selfish living streaming across
the globe and to be found around
many a table, snatching what's
there with greedy hands and more,
connected to lives made empty —

A Common Folly

. . . looking for something more
in places that offer what is less

(so much less) . . .

Ready for Over

How often man continues to do things
in ways that are obsolete, using methods
that have had their day (well passé)
working ever harder at what can no longer
deliver as it used to, ready for the trash heap,
failing to meet the demands of the present
hour, yet man persists like a canine looking
up at a dying tree, refusing to move from
the object of its attention, still standing
but never to function the way it once did
(near to lifeless, giving all it was able to give)
as the expectation remains that it will be as
it has always been, the reality ignored that
its days of usefulness are behind it, its purpose
now all but gone with nothing to come but
the downing, and the need to move on —

and man stays where he is . . . goes on
trying . . . (barking) . . .

A Mocking Farce

Many are sacrificed to the Machine of
Corruption to hold in place what is falling
of its own weight, crumbling like a poorly
designed tower of ancient times which
nothing in modern times can keep standing
but the sweat and blood of millions
lubing the giant gears that have caused
so many tears (rivers of tears) and held
the ideal of freedom to a mocking farce

The sacred promise betrayed, going down
and under

Destructive Path

The destructive path laid by destructive
natures followed by the weak of mind and
character, heading to what can only be disaster —
and the leaders die on the path, the followers
die on the path, replaced with new leaders and
followers, the path long (so long) going back
(way back) paved centuries ago by the shortest
sights of vision and basest of values carrying
the scourge of false principles to bring ruin upon
ruin, though the path be taken and again to be
taken in numbers as high as the path is low
in the intervals between the upheavals
never to bring something more, to manifest
anything different than what greed and
cruelty and injustice and fraudulence and
turpitude and bigotry can ever produce —

Spread of False Tutelage

There is no sun there, in those days
of battered youth; only the dark shade
of a moon in a sky where nothing is held
to scrutiny's light; and battered not
worse by fist and calloused tongue, but by
a preconditioning and imposition of ways
rooted in the soil of iniquity successfully
advertised and accepted as being good,
right, respectable (even noble) — the
spread of false tutelage injected into
the veins of youth, sending poison
unfiltered into the future —

Motion Empty

You see the masses in a confused mass
of empty motion and you know their way
is not the way to go [just can't be the way],
that it is a death sentence with the first step
but still you are drawn to it in a strange
way but know you must break with it,
must turn away from it, stay clear of it
and be clear in head and heart about the
way of it, about the sentence of death that
it is given, leading to death before dying —

Truth Be Told

Truth be told, much truth goes
untold, much truth is distorted
much truth is aborted in this
less-than-truthful world —

Once More

A sleight of brilliance, like
champagne bottles uncorked
foaming over the top, missing
the glasses on Faith's table
soaking the cloth leaving
the guests thirsting again, to
be kept once more from the
promise that hasn't been kept

Off the Record

... That's where the good stuff is —
the better stuff — the real stuff...
Falsehood not standing guard —
The truth being revealed raw and
uncensored, leaving some raw and
(post revealment) moving to censor —

Another Deficit

Life gives more than
enough to think about
for every human head
but not every human
head is a thinking head
and so much of what Is
is never thought about
and what is is never
enough

Priceless Loss

Lots of things in this world, and
people too can distract you, can
sidetrack you, can derail you if you
let them [and many do let them]
and a price is paid rarely recognized
at the time of the interference/
interruption where energy
[invaluable] is squandered
[irretrievable] and the same of
course with time that is gone
forever and for nothing and the
story is repeated many times over
[the number of times not seeming
to diminish no matter the number of
warnings] and the joy song of youth
becomes the sad song of age when
too many younger days have been
frittered away, when the bait was
foolishly taken that took one off
the unique path that was one's own,
that could have given one's life the
meaning and purpose one had so
longed for and life calls for,
never to be known —

Needing the Work

Throughout the world work is being
done that is deemed necessary (even
crucial) to meet the needs of survival;
humans working a job to get by,
something that keeps them afloat
[materially alive] and more there are
who need a different kind of work,
a spiritual work [the inner work]
not being done in their lives, not
realizing how much they are
dying inside . . .

[how much they need the work]

Until Turning Away

The world turns no matter
what we do and what we do
doesn't matter [can never
matter] until turning away
from the round and round
of it all, getting off the spin —

Time and Again

Dreamers there are and part-time
enthusiasts getting themselves all
worked up, most excited about what
will never happen because they don't
realize at the time of the exhilaration
that they really don't want to do the
work required to make it happen
(wanting the prize without the effort)
and they make big plans and talk big
talk and experience exalted feelings
and delight in how good it's going to be . . .

[the thing that will never happen]

The Inauthentic

They hide in their careers, they hide
in their traditions, they hide in their
social and political associations; they
hide in their cultures, their biases, their
conventions, their tribal inclinations
to family and religion; they hide in all
they dare not question [fail to question]
giving nothing fresh to life [no oxygen,
no blood], running even when walking
out and about in the open, leaving
themselves unopened —

Only Smoke

A fire is fed, kept alive, yet
delivers only smoke . . .
True this is, in the literal sense
but also in the figurative . . .
able to match with myriads
of endeavors in the temporal —

Hence wise it is to pause and
consider before stoking a fire,
before efforts are made to keep
something going that can only
deliver smoke —

Not the Better World

Something's always getting the better
of something that's better than what
it is that is getting the better of it —
but only in the temporal world . . .

(Which isn't the better world)

Sad Display

All the eyes that see nothing
the ears that hear nothing
the tongues that say nothing
the minds preoccupied with such
that is as good as thinking nothing
the actions that do nothing
the hope that leads to nothing
as Life (abounding Life)
is being passed by
by life after life
just passing by

. . .

As Time Goes On

As time goes on there is more
and more talk and less and
less thought which causes the
world an increase of suffering
with many too busy talking
or texting to think about
thinking about this —

At a Crossway

Standing at a crossway waiting for
the traffic light to change, watching
vehicles passing through the square with
driver after driver holding a cell phone
to an ear with one hand and the other
hand on the steering wheel, the mouths
of some motorists moving [talking]
while others appear to be listening
(or just waiting for their turn to speak) —
a show of traffic giving a parade of mobile
communication (a favorite modern day
fashion on display) and a curiosity enters
the moment of how much light there is in
the words/phrases/'thoughts' of the drivers
celling while driving in the close-to-midday
traffic noisily rolling on —

Store Encounter

Stopped at a supermarket for a
few items . . . many people there,
more than customary given the
day and time (having to do with
a snow blizzard on the way);
stood in line longer than usual
next to an elderly man
he said he didn't want to be there
his wife made him go
I talked about the human race
getting weaker and more unstable
he talked about the coffee he liked
I told him we were headed for
major catastrophe
he said he couldn't find the cheese
his wife told him to buy
I said disaster was ready to strike
from all directions
he said he wasn't sure if the cake mix he
pointed to in his cart was the right brand
I bid him goodbye at the checkout counter
he disputed the price of a head of lettuce
with the girl at the register

The wind picking up outside —

Crashing Before Light

. . . and then the world promised to get
itself together, and the wind turned to
howling laughter, and the fire turned
away from the bush burning only itself
and cruelty turned to kindness and hatred
to love, and clouds ever gave way to the
sun and peace was the default of the globe
and the grace of beauty and wisdom
illuminated the dark, and the hope for
mass enlightenment came flooding into
being and sense was made of everything

and then the dream ended and the realities
of this world came crashing into head
and gut before light —

For All It's Worth

Truth can do a number on
your nerves (no doubt)
but what can one be worth
(be about) if one hasn't
the courage (the nerve)
to take it on and take it in
for all it's worth . . . .

        (W
         h
         a
         t)

     [? ? ?]

What Few Seem to Realize

In a psychological jungle fraught with
danger is where life drops those off who
look to get to the best of it, like a special
ops mission to free themselves if they can
[if they dare] from the many demons of
illusion that hold the power of reality
until recognized to be illusion —

[and you thought it would be a safe safari
sponsored by Disneyland . . .]

Removing the Chance

Removed is the chance from
their lives of getting to the magic
who think good things will happen
for them and humankind alike
just like that without good effort
behind the arrival of their happening

. . . . [Just like magic]

Like Keys to a Car

How easily have those of numbers not few
turned the keys of their lives over to others . . .
as easy as surrendering the keys to their
cars when not caring to drive, forfeiting
command of the direction of their course —
and how difficult to face the cost of repairs
that so often accrues from handing over
to another what should have always been
theirs to command — [and theirs alone]
. . .

Waiting Without Doing

All this waiting . . . waiting without
doing; expecting it to happen
(many 'its' to happen); the vacuity
of effort/work/action not being filled
(not happening) due to sloth and
ineptitude and throw fear into the mix
(that too) which brings Hope on the
scene to sit by Expectation, ready to sit
for years, for decades if that's the way
it will be —

Something's Gotta Give

in a world of the uncommitted, of the
unwilling, in this world falling ever short
in the ways of giving; in these lands of
spiritual desolation, of weighty monuments
raised in praise of mediocrity; in this age
of incapacity with its stranglehold of
ignorance around new generations
plagued by a dearth of curiosity and
discipline; in this time of the braveless,
spoiling the face of nobility and taking
all the spoils

Oh yes . . . . . Something

An Invitation

The feeling of out-of-placeness is
an inner call, an invitation to freedom,
the offering of something strong,
more powerful than what can be
known to the right-at-homers
never to hit a life homer from
the field of the ephemeral, feeling
at ease in their belonging, adjusted
well to the cage that keeps them
societally tranquil and spiritually
dead

Not Starting the Life

Through countless days
people start their days going
day after day, up till their
final day into their final hour
without ever having started the
life to make it all worthwhile

Better than Play

While many are looking forward to their next
day off, the artist looks forward to his next day
on — when things are coming together through
a surge of inspiration accompanied by a creativity
powering an inner force, coming out with the goods —
the work going well and strong, with the output
high; and he hopes that the next day on will be the
day that follows, and the day after that — would
like it to be every day [all his life's tomorrows] —
and though not to be [for anyone, it just couldn't be]
he knows on those special days, the joy of a certain
kind of work that outdoes that of any kind of play
to be had on any 'day off' that many throughout
their days of work will hold in their minds to be
among the engagements prized most in their lives . . .
days to ever look forward to —

A Stirring Warmth

It is a cold day today . . .
cold, but bright and beautiful
lighting through the morning
air, stirring an inner warmth
like the stoking of a spiritual
fireplace, all senses of awakening
now rising from their beds . . .

Sight and Sounds of Joy

There is a hollow in the roof above the residence
below that I can see outside my window, and
when it rains it fills with water and sometimes
birds arrive, especially when the rain subsides
to drink and splash about for a while before
flying away, which is nothing remarkable —
But once I saw a robin inside the opening
holding a small pool of water, batting its wings
and moving its head down and up, down and up
taking water in its beak and when its thirst
was satisfied, it lifted its head to the sky and
started to sing with quivering breast and wings
now fluttering with blinding speed — the bird
looking joyous and sounding joyous, projecting a
joy I swear I could feel coming through the walls
and it went on for some time in that moment
of trackless time, and then it flew away as a
thought came to mind of how many humans
will likely never know or experience a time of
blissful abandon like that bird just had —

(how sad)

To Capture the Fury

Strange day it was in this small part of the
globe; starting calm, barely a breeze, sunny —
then shortly past noon the winds picked up,
rising quickly to a sixty-mile-per-hour force
gusting snow from the sky and that of previous
snowfalls lying about in the region swept up by
the gales, and soon after [not two minutes later],
it was over — the calm and sunlight returning
as before . . . strange, that is, in the manner of
change without warning and just as sudden
return to the climatic condition of the morning
hours raising the thought that such a visit
from the Muse is not as unusual; taking one
by surprise with its sudden arrival and measure
of force more often when it comes than the
meteorological happening of the above, passing
through mind and spirit with what it came
to deliver, and then gone — but what is left,
vivid, demanding an attention and awareness
of a degree beyond the norm . . . one then
picking up the tools of one's artistry as quickly
as the rising of the winds to get to work . . .
to capture the fury —

And So the Artist

Whatever goes on outside of it,
whatever makes war or generates
peace, Nature keeps doing its thing —

And so the artist of a thousand dreams

The Thinkerman

The thinkerman like the fisherman
coming in after a long day's work,
out on the oceans of the earth
the thinkerman out in the oceans
of the mind bringing home the day's
catch, rejoicing if landing a good
day's bounty, and wondering
what tomorrow will bring —

How Many (Minds) at Work

A sign I see (another sign) that reads "men
at work"; this phrase, positioned to be read
many times on any day on many streets
and it triggers a memory of once passing by
such a traffic warning and wondering how
many minds were at work at that moment,
truly *at work* making roads [pathways] into
a future [a possible future] of light and truth
and power times power, on the trail of
something revolutionary; I wondered if
the number was even as high as that of the
signs that had the "men at work" caution
or something similar posted on streets
that morning around the world; minds
doing the most serious kind of cerebral work
reaching beyond the transient, exerting efforts
being built upon to one day deliver something
of the profound, something transcending the
passing of time . . . how many, I wondered
. . .

No Preparation

How often in the human world have plans
been made to engage in serious work then
put off, planned again, and again put off by
innocents only to discover when finally
settling down to the task in front of an
empty page in a notepad or computer, or
standing before a canvas or other apparatus
for creative endeavor, the reality that they
have nothing to say; nothing of interest
coming to mind . . . void of inspiration;
no ideas or deep sentiments to mine — not
understanding that such work requires
much preparation; lots of time alone, thinking,
and more thinking . . . which deepens feeling,
which together with a deepening of thought
creates its own momentum of creativity . . .
this vital part of what produces substantive
work [most essential] is not present for the
one who is ever putting aside, postponing
what he said he really wanted to do, what he
was truly about; allowing distractions to get
in the way of what was believed to be his life's
passion, the disappointing truth that serious
work requires serious commitment that
begins long before the work begins, ever

in play, with no one getting around it . . .
[no one to put it aside] —

Cusp of Change

On the cusp of change
[profound change]
everything seems
to go still
like a quiet
that's never been
before in a place
that never was

No One Else

They sit in a hall with pen and paper
in hand, there before a motivational
speaker (as one is called) listening more
intently than they have ever listened to
themselves, scratching words on a page
that will tell them how to improve their
lives, the way to give them direction;
how to make them more vibrant and
productive, and just watch them take flight
if you take his advice . . . needing to hear
something, to listen to someone other
than themselves for a guidance that can
never take them farther than to the end
of the proverbial block, for what they are
searching for is nowise to be attained
until the inner block is removed that
keeps them from looking inward,
allowing for an exploration within
to find the answers to their lives
that no one else can ever give them —

Silence

is the repose
is the response
is the refuge
is the freedom space
is the power center
of true power,
the cover without cover;
is the timeless realm
and peace of time,
is the exit from temporal causation,
the entrance to eternal affirmation;
is the womb of all creation

Some Would Say

Human contact is good [and
can be nice] some would say
important, but not as important
[some would say] as making
contact with that inner power
and light that make such
light work of the temporal
and laugh in the face of death —

You Said

I will work
I will create
I will advance
I will transform
I will move to the countryside
of my life and inhale the breath of
sweet silence and awaken the
angels of my soul . . . .

The countryside is still waiting,
and the angels are still asleep

And So It Goes

Ever trying to find meaning are seekers
looking to where it doesn't exist and deny
themselves from having it by not understanding
that they need to play a part in its creation
[which is the only way for meaning in their
lives to be had] but this is something many
deny [just won't buy] as they continue their
search for what they will never find because
the focus of the quest is external [their biggest
mistake] staying clear of the journey that
[yes] causes pain, but also brings gain
[the only true gain] from which everything
worthwhile can be discovered/created/given,
wrapped in light of the Eternal . . .
[the gift of true meaning] —

In Human Form

To not leave this life before it is time to depart . . .
not realize [deeply sense] that this temporal
existence wants us out the door like a lingering
guest who has overstayed his welcome . . . to
not venture outside its dwellings, turning
away from the exit leading to the entrance of
Life where resides the Wonder of all wonders,
the way to something greater [so much more],
is to be at the end like someone taken away
after breathing his last at the table of an inn,
having spent too much time in its confines,
never going beyond its vicinity, out and over
the hills to what beckons the human spirit to
the Light of all light, the Power of all power,
to be welcomed into the Eternal Now, in
human form —

Do Not Bind Yourself

Do not bind yourself —
No, do not bind yourself to this world —
Not to this world or the things of this world —
Do not bind yourself . . .
Do not bind yourself to the goals of death,
to the illusions and dead ends of temporality;
No, do not bind —
Not even yourself to your life,
or to the story of your life;
Do not bind yourself . . .
And do not bind others to yourself;
And seek not to stand in the sun as it
is going down,
do not give yourself to this descent;
But do give of yourself (of your being) and
what emanates from the higher planes of your being . . .
Yes, do give of this without boundness to anything,
for to give without binding is to give without end —
Is to give all that can be given . . .
For the sake of all

Here

to measure up;
Here, to take the fire;
Here, to give heat
and to raise the heat;
Here, to break the ice,
Here, to brave the dark,
Here to take it up a notch;
Here to earn the courage for
the light of truth;
Here, to be a mind explorer
to be a spirit explorer
to be a human explorer of the
human phenomenon;
to not shy away from
discipline, from sacrifice;
to shun all compromise that destroys
the promise of the noble heart;
Here to stay the path of transcendence . . .
There to the final end —

What It Was All About

Will you keep going, not give up; see the journey
through, even when unsure of where you are going
but feeling positive that *there's something more*, and
not lose heart in those darkest periods that seem
like they'll last forever, and nothing appears to be
going well/good/right for you and jeers are coming
at you from quarters that haven't a clue of what
you're about or trying to do . . . if so, and if the
journey is true and travelled far enough within,
a realm is entered that you never knew was there,
filled with treasure, like coming upon a lost tomb
of an ancient pharaoh, *only better* — discovering
a wealth beyond measure, like nothing the material
world can provide . . . this, the reason for the cost,
the challenge, the test of it all; what it was truly
about; uncovered only because you didn't give up
(give in, give out) . . . and now comes a new life
rich in light and greater love raising the experience
of Being to a dynamic heretofore unknown, to be
lived with rejoice and gratitude for what has been
found, and a yearning to continue the work of discovery
and the fulfillment of possibilities yet to be achieved.

ABOUT THE AUTHOR

Carroll Blair is an award-winning author of more than twenty books. His work has been well endorsed and commendably reviewed, as illustrated by the following commentary from Midwest Review, which proclaimed, *"The poetic expression of Carroll Blair is both unique and compelling. Using word images like the strokes of a painter's brush, Blair creates a resonating recognition that is the mark of a master poet."* He is an alumnus of the Boston Conservatory and lives in Massachusetts.